Southern COOKING

Desserts
CONTENTS

New Orleans-Style Pralines

MAKES ABOUT 34 PRALINES (1¼ POUNDS)

2 cups packed brown sugar

1 cup half-and-half

½ teaspoon salt

2 tablespoons butter

2 tablespoons bourbon or cognac *or* 1 teaspoon vanilla

1 package (10 ounces) chopped pecans (about 2½ cups), toasted

1 Line two baking sheets with parchment paper or foil. Combine brown sugar, half-and-half and salt in heavy medium saucepan. Cook over medium heat until sugar is dissolved and mixture begins to boil, stirring occasionally.

2 Clip candy thermometer to side of pan, making sure bulb is submerged in sugar mixture but not touching bottom of pan. Continue boiling about 20 minutes until sugar mixture reaches soft-ball stage (235° to 240°F) on candy thermometer, stirring occasionally. (Watch carefully; candy will be grainy if overcooked.) Remove from heat; stir in butter and bourbon. Stir in pecans.

3 Working quickly, drop mixture by tablespoonfuls onto prepared baking sheets. (If mixture becomes too thick, stir in 1 to 2 teaspoons hot water and reheat over medium heat.) Cool completely, about 30 minutes. Store in airtight container at room temperature up to 3 days.

Strawberry Rhubarb Pie

MAKES 8 SERVINGS

Double-Crust Pie Pastry
(recipe follows)

1½ cups granulated sugar

½ cup cornstarch

2 tablespoons quick-cooking
tapioca

1 tablespoon grated lemon peel

¼ teaspoon ground allspice

4 cups sliced rhubarb (1-inch
pieces)

3 cups sliced fresh strawberries

1 egg, lightly beaten

Coarse sugar (optional)

1 Prepare Double-Crust Pie Pastry. Preheat oven to 425°F. Roll out one pastry disc into 11-inch circle on floured surface. Line 9-inch pie plate with pastry; flute edge.

2 Combine granulated sugar, cornstarch, tapioca, lemon peel and allspice in large bowl. Add rhubarb and strawberries; toss to coat. Pour into crust.

3 Roll out remaining pastry disc into 10-inch circle; cut into ½-inch-wide strips. Arrange in lattice design over fruit, tucking in ends. Seal and flute edge. Brush pastry with beaten egg and sprinkle with coarse sugar, if desired.

4 Bake 50 minutes or until filling is thick and bubbly and crust is golden brown. Cool on wire rack. Serve warm or at room temperature.

Double-Crust Pie Pastry

Combine 2½ cups all-purpose flour, 1 teaspoon salt and 1 teaspoon granulated sugar in large bowl. Cut in 1 cup (2 sticks) cubed unsalted butter with pastry blender or two knives until mixture resembles coarse crumbs. Drizzle ⅓ cup ice water over flour mixture, 2 tablespoons at a time, stirring just until dough comes together. Divide dough in half. Shape each half into a disc; wrap in plastic wrap. Refrigerate 30 minutes.

Hermits

MAKES ABOUT 4 DOZEN COOKIES

6 tablespoons (¾ stick) unsalted butter, softened

¼ cup packed dark brown sugar

1 egg

1 package (about 15 ounces) yellow cake mix

⅓ cup molasses

1 teaspoon ground cinnamon

¼ teaspoon baking soda

¾ cup raisins

¾ cup chopped pecans

2½ tablespoons maple syrup

1 tablespoon butter, melted

¼ teaspoon maple flavoring

¾ cup powdered sugar

1 Preheat oven to 375°F. Line cookie sheets with parchment paper.

2 Beat softened butter and brown sugar in large bowl with electric mixer at medium speed until well blended. Beat in egg. Add cake mix, molasses, cinnamon and baking soda; beat just until blended. Stir in raisins and pecans. Drop dough by rounded tablespoonfuls 1½ inches apart onto prepared cookie sheets.

3 Bake 13 to 15 minutes or until set. Cool on cookie sheets 5 minutes. Remove to wire racks; cool completely.

4 Combine maple syrup, melted butter and maple flavoring in medium bowl. Add powdered sugar, ¼ cup at a time, stirring until smooth. Spread glaze over cookies; let stand 30 minutes or until set.

Sweet Potato Crumb Cake

MAKES 6 CAKES

Crumb Topping
½ cup granulated sugar
Grated peel of 1 orange
1 teaspoon ground cinnamon
½ cup chopped pecans
¼ cup all-purpose flour
¼ cup old-fashioned oats

¼ cup (½ stick) cold butter, cut into 4 pieces

Cake
1 package (16 ounces) sweet potato pound cake mix, plus ingredients to prepare mix
Powdered sugar (optional)

1 Preheat oven to 350°F. Spray six individual loaf pans with nonstick cooking spray.

2 Combine granulated sugar and orange peel in food processor; pulse several times to thoroughly mix. Add cinnamon and pecans; pulse until pecans are size of peas. Reserve ⅓ cup of crumb mixture; set aside.

3 Add flour, oats and butter to remaining crumb mixture in food processor; pulse until mixture resembles coarse crumbs.

4 Prepare cake mix according to package directions. Divide batter in half. Evenly pour one half into prepared pans. Evenly sprinkle with ⅓ cup reserved crumb mixture. Spoon remaining batter evenly over crumb mixture. Top with oat crumb mixture.

5 Bake 25 to 30 minutes or until toothpick inserted into centers comes out clean. Cool in pans 15 minutes. Remove to wire rack; cool completely. Dust with powdered sugar, if desired.

Honey Gingersnaps

MAKES 3½ DOZEN COOKIES

2 cups all-purpose flour

1 tablespoon ground ginger

2 teaspoons baking soda

½ teaspoon salt

⅛ teaspoon ground cloves

½ cup shortening

¼ cup (½ stick) butter, softened

1½ cups sugar, divided

¼ cup honey

1 egg

1 teaspoon vanilla

1 Preheat oven to 350°F. Line cookie sheets with parchment paper. Combine flour, ginger, baking soda, salt and cloves in medium bowl.

2 Beat shortening and butter in large bowl with electric mixer at medium speed until smooth. Gradually beat in 1 cup sugar until blended; increase speed to high and beat until light and fluffy. Beat in honey, egg and vanilla until fluffy. Gradually stir in flour mixture until blended.

3 Shape dough into 1-inch balls. Place remaining ½ cup sugar in shallow bowl; roll balls in sugar to coat. Place 2 inches apart on prepared cookie sheets.

4 Bake 10 minutes or until golden brown. Cool on cookie sheets 5 minutes. Remove to wire racks; cool completely. Store in airtight container up to 1 week.

Banana Pudding Squares

MAKES 18 SERVINGS

1 cup graham cracker crumbs

2 tablespoons butter, melted

1 package (8 ounces) cream cheese, softened

3 cups milk

2 packages (4-serving size each) banana cream instant pudding and pie filling mix

1 container (8 ounces) whipped topping, divided

2 medium bananas

1 Line 13×9-inch baking pan with foil; spray with nonstick cooking spray.

2 Combine graham cracker crumbs and butter in small bowl; stir until well blended. Press into bottom of prepared pan.

3 Beat cream cheese in large bowl with electric mixer at low speed until smooth. Add milk and pudding mixes; beat at high speed 2 minutes or until smooth and creamy. Fold in half of whipped topping until well blended. Spread half of pudding mixture over crust.

4 Peel bananas; cut into ¼-inch slices. Arrange bananas evenly over pudding layer. Spoon remaining pudding mixture over bananas; spread remaining whipped topping evenly over pudding mixture.

5 Cover loosely with plastic wrap; refrigerate 2 hours or up to 8 hours.

Apple-Pear Praline Pie

MAKES 8 SERVINGS

Double-Crust Pie Pastry
(page 6)

4 cups sliced peeled Granny
Smith apples

2 cups sliced peeled pears

¾ cup granulated sugar

¼ cup plus 1 tablespoon
all-purpose flour, divided

4 teaspoons ground cinnamon

¼ teaspoon salt

½ cup (1 stick) plus
2 tablespoons butter,
divided

1 cup packed brown sugar

1 tablespoon half-and-half or
milk

1 cup chopped pecans

1   Prepare Double-Crust Pie Pastry.

2   Combine apples, pears, granulated sugar, ¼ cup flour, cinnamon and salt in large bowl; toss to coat. Let stand 15 minutes.

3   Preheat oven to 350°F. Roll out one disc of pastry into 11-inch circle on floured surface. Line deep-dish 9-inch pie plate with pastry; sprinkle with remaining 1 tablespoon flour. Spoon fruit mixture into crust; dot with 2 tablespoons butter. Roll out remaining disc of pastry into 10-inch circle. Place over fruit; seal and flute edge. Cut slits in top crust.

4   Bake 1 hour. Meanwhile, combine remaining ½ cup butter, brown sugar and half-and-half in small saucepan; bring to a boil over medium heat, stirring frequently. Boil 2 minutes, stirring constantly. Remove from heat; stir in pecans. Spread over pie.

5   Cool pie on wire rack at least 20 minutes. Serve warm or at room temperature.

Fudgy Marshmallow Popcorn

MAKES ABOUT 15 CUPS

3½ quarts popped popcorn (about 14 cups)

2 cups sugar

1 cup evaporated milk

¼ cup (½ stick) butter

1 cup (½ of 7-ounce jar) marshmallow creme

1 cup semisweet chocolate chips

1 teaspoon vanilla

1 Spray baking sheets with nonstick cooking spray or line with parchment paper. Place popcorn in large bowl.

2 Combine sugar, evaporated milk and butter in medium saucepan. Cook over medium heat until sugar is dissolved and mixture comes to a boil, stirring constantly. Boil 5 minutes. Remove from heat. Stir in marshmallow creme, chocolate chips and vanilla until chocolate is melted and mixture is smooth.

3 Pour chocolate mixture over popcorn, stirring until completely coated. Spread in single layer on prepared baking sheets. Refrigerate until set.